In reading these poems I know I'm being guided by a poet who's maintained control. These poems are marvelously condensed, and fine attention has been paid to each word.

SARAH MANGUSO,
AUTHOR OF *300 ARGUMENTS* AND *ONGOINGNESS: THE END OF A DIARY*

In her collection, *Shelter in Place*, Catherine Kyle offers unapologetic mirrors and terrifying prophecies; these graceful, imaginative poems are not afraid to look into the deep dark—within and without—into the places we often close our eyes against. Refusing retreat, spurning sanctuary, Kyle's poetry is interrogatory, seeking answers: if we advocate awareness as a "balm," especially now "in the age of the image," how can we stare into the faces of suffering and do nothing? She goes on to ask: "if this world is a story, / what is its moral," an answer that relies on our acceptance of responsibility as "the sovereign or the heir." Will we be parent or legacy, liberator or disciple? Kyle reminds us that although we often give in—make deals with crossroads demons, relinquish our "hands" for "gloves," the "softest kid skin," take the easy outs—through it all we have a choice; we can choose to be museums, to "make shelters of / our bodies," to "carry the ghosts / of what is lost." We can "become custom jobs," play our parts, save empathy, create change. Even as Kyle's poetry terrifies and punctures us with worry, it rebels, refusing to relinquish hope, goading us into bravery. *Shelter in Place* is a warning, a slap in the face, a kick in the ass, a pre-apocalyptic prayer, a guide to action where "agency" equals "lullaby elegy power."

KARA DORRIS,
AUTHOR OF *NIGHT RIDE HOME* AND *UNTITLED FILM STILL MUSEUM*

In *Shelter in Place*, Catherine Kyle gracefully captures the voice of a generation unwilling to ignore that it inherited a damaged world, skillfully illuminating what it means to be truly observant and aware in our media-driven culture. Her witty, imaginative poems seamlessly navigate the fragility of our relationships with ourselves, each other, and the earth, reminding us how technology both connects and disconnects us. *Shelter in Place* is a delightful read, a timely, thoughtful collection.

HANNAH RODABAUGH,
AUTHOR OF *WE DON'T BURY OUR DEAD WHEN OUR DEAD ARE ANIMALS* AND *WITH WORDS: VERSE IN CONCORDANCE*

With the knowledge that humanity faces probable extinction while most of us are unable, and some unwilling, to prevent it, Catherine Kyle has done the only thing that makes any sense to me: she's written a book of spells. The poems in *Shelter in Place* possess the power to galvanize the many witches and warlocks living in our cities, our cyberspaces, and everywhere there are people. I am grateful for the author's generous wit and willingness to stare unflinching into severe realities. For as long as I continue to live under the gargantuan thumb of capitalism, on hard days this book shall provide a fine complement, and on brighter days an alternative, to despair.

WILLIAM HOFFACKER,
EDITOR OF *CARTRIDGE LIT*

Catherine Kyle's *Shelter in Place* lyricizes the Cold War between seductive robots and anxious screen-eaters. Come sit in the glow of digital preoccupation; Kyle has planted an uncanny garden of pixels.

CHRISTINE SLOAN STODDARD, AUTHOR OF *BELLADONNA MAGIC* AND *WATER FOR THE CACTUS WOMAN*

Shelter in Place

Shelter in Place

Catherine Kyle

Spuyten Duyvil
New York City

ACKNOWLEDGMENTS

Gratitude is extended to the editors of the journals in which the following pieces appeared, some in slightly different forms:

Eunoia Review: "Embedded," "Word of the Year," "The Age of the Image," "Shortcuts," "Datum," and "Prayer."
Occulum: "Boss Fight" and "Blossoming 1."
Quail Bell Magazine: "Seven Reasons to Have Hope for a Better Future. Number Five Will Really Get You!" and "Thread 2."
Rag Queen Periodical: "Adaptable" and "Tarot Reading for the End of the World."
Rise Up Review: "Suspicion."
Venefica Magazine: "Apotropaic" was first published in *Venefica*, Vol./Issue 2, by Melissa Madara and published by Catland Books, LLC.
Yes, Poetry: "Dear Phantom Children" and "Geode-Eaters."

Thank you to Zach, Diane, Jason, Hannah, Megan, and Carl for their invaluable feedback on these poems. Thank you to Katie, David, Lessie, Ryan, Emily, and many other friends for encouraging and inspiring me along the way. Thank you, also, to the directors of the Alexa Rose Foundation and the Two Eight Residency, who helped nurture the roots of this work. Finally, thank you to the faculty and students of New England College's MFA program for their encouragement, care, and attention to this manuscript; and to the editors of Spuyten Duyvil for believing in it and giving it a home.

© 2019 Catherine Kyle
ISBN 978-1-949966-40-4
Cover photo by Simon Zhu.

Library of Congress Cataloging-in-Publication Data

Names: Kyle, Catherine, author.
Title: Shelter in place / Catherine Kyle.
Description: New York City : Spuyten Duyvil, [2019] | Summary: "Poems regarding emergency shelter-seeking"-- Provided by publisher.
Identifiers: LCCN 2019022904 | ISBN 9781949966404 (paperback)
Classification: LCC PS3611.Y56 A6 2019 | DDC 811/.6--dc23
LC record available at https://lccn.loc.gov/2019022904

*For L., J., and C.,
companions and friends*

CONTENTS

Bunker

Commute 3

Dear Phantom Children 4

Mallard 6

Candle and Laptop 7

Seven Reasons to Have Hope for a Better Future.
    Number Five Will Really Get You! 9

Adaptable 11

Faith 12

Tarot Reading for the End of the World 13

Geode-Eaters 15

Apotropaic 16

Morals 18

Ordinary Magic 19

Narratives 20

Embedded 21

Thread 1 22

Fortress

Fever Dream 27

Word of the Year 30

Shrug 31

Personality Test 32

The Age of the Image 35

Paywall 36

Moloch 1 37

Moloch 2   39

Personhood   40

Made for You   41

Online Forum   42

Boss Fight   44

Shortcuts   45

Thread 2   46

Siege

Through the Cracks   51

Blossoming 1   52

Blossoming 2   53

The Squeeze   54

Advice   55

Discordant   56

Suspicion   57

Datum   58

Museums   59

Trivia   60

Communion with Nature   61

Prayer   62

Thread 3   63

NOTES   68

One of the instructions you may be given in an emergency where hazardous materials may have been released into the atmosphere is to shelter-in-place. This is a precaution aimed to keep you safe while remaining indoors. (This is not the same thing as going to a shelter in case of a storm.) Shelter-in-place means selecting a small, interior room, with no or few windows, and taking refuge there.

[…]

Bring your pets with you.

> —"Fact Sheet on Shelter-in-Place," American Red Cross

Bunker

COMMUTE

Good tidings enter—through ear
-bud, through cracked screen.

The city, its glitter pulse holy egg
gold, a feasting of steel on

birds. By this, we mean humans
in cable cars, electric blue snapping

each bend in the track, thumbs
stroking ineffable feeds. This

is a custom job—phone case
unique as the nape that lowers

toward it. Don't mind the plastic
is sourced from the same vat

as that one, and that one, and that.
Don't mind the circuits obey the same

patent. Don't mind the logo transfusing
your face as you gaze out the smog

-kissed shuffling glass. Its fluorescent
letters curlicuing your eyes. Its underscore

stitching your lips. *We* do not mind
this. Listen: the next good tidings will play

right after this ad. Will singe
the skyline saffron. As if a sudden

paper cut, as if the sun
bleeds light.

Dear Phantom Children

Dear phantom children
who hover near the futon frame

like lavender genies or wisps
of feathered incense smoke, take heed—

we get it. You enjoy the look
of daffodils and jello. It might be fun

to dress you as a puppy or a cub. We've pushed
our share of strollers watching neighbor ladies'

babies, and yes, the dappling of sun on plaid
and board book can be sweet. The thing is,

spirits, we can barely even hold each other—
our other hands latched to the railing of this speeding ship.

*

To those already here, well, welcome
to the holey vessel. We'll do our best

to patch it up before it's sink or
kill. We're trying not to polar bear

ourselves or leave you ice cubes
from which you'll have to hop and

hop, precarious wayfare. Democracy,
the ultimate hair-tearing-out group project.

Humanity, the raft that everybody wants
to steer. For now, don't worry, babies; look—

aurora borealis. Take a load off, babies; look
at Ursa Major rise.

Mallard

Walking past a building named Mallard,
we wince to see a duck

demolished, lying in the gutter. A sprig
of down catches our eyes, and like a constellation,

the image unfolds: his feathery sternum, entirety
intact. Green head shimmering, a forest flecked

with snow. Wings outstretched, a dirty angel
tangled in rust leaves. We could almost

lift him up, say, *This
is the body. This is the sacrifice.* Could name

the children saved by this as we draw
the cross in the air with our hands: Industry,

Avarice, Alacrity, Sprawl. Could almost sing, *Amen,*
but look, the crosswalk light has changed.

Candle and Laptop

Our succulents poised on apartment windowsills
suction the starlight again. Are open as nocturnal

waterlilies, drinking the arid dusk. Are accustomed
to living on little. Have taken root, a set of stubborn

fingers lodged in clay. Pearly green as misty jasper
bruised with blushing road rash orange. Vermillion

and rust. We water their spines with Mason jars
we saved from eating jelly. The sink staccato, pooling

drips, a silver basin decked with buttercup and agate
blue: twin submersion of candle and laptop casting

errant glow. The city is enough with us, has had
its bite today. We swim home, salmon gnawed-on,

gored by seals' frothy grins. The city is a neon flashing
predatory pulse. Something whose heat we feel

beside us, raising the hair on our arms. But we are home
now, pulling up self-care on screens and screens and

screens. Our cats are breathing near our feet. Our tea
issues its gauzy steam, its pointillism puffs. When we

were young, the rumor was that all our cats should
be kept in, that teenagers on Halloween would catch

and crucify them. Maybe just a rumor, but
the world is full of them. By this, we mean

real bastards, so we always shut the door. Even when
we're only ferrying garbage to the curb. Any of our

many screens can conjure facts on such cats, the way
old superstitions equate them with witch words. So

we shelter what we can. We shelter the cat,
her licked whiskers. We bunker in the glow of buttercup

and agate blue. When we extinguish these by breath
or fold the shiny screens closed, we trace our way

by trusting lunar auras in the sky. We slumber through
the screech and breaking hymns outside

our windows. We nestle in our pillow forts, pairs
of ribs tidal in time until the walls sing rose.

Seven Reasons to Have Hope for a Better Future. Number Five Will Really Get You!

And lo the beast said unto us, *Persuade me*
    not to carnage

this world by the jugular. Inform me
    why I care. And we responded, *Avocado*

toast in bed with lovers. We responded, *Instagramming*
    fatal ideation

with a photograph of berries
    emptied from a bag. Caption: "Bummer, all

my summer berries have been whiplashed
    through with freezer burn," and having friends

know what we mean. We responded, *Having friends*
    send double heart emojis; calling us—"Are you

okay?"—and meeting for
    takeout. We responded, *Dairy-free and gluten-free*

small pizzas, little sensitivities
    that business can survive. In other words,

the notion that the globe is complicated. In other words,
    the notion that it's not hard to be kind. We responded, *Eyeliner*

not made from crushed-up fish fins. We resist
    economies of grindery and pain. We responded, *Human*

things, the glittering of twilight
    laughter out the Buick window, night rushing our hands.

We responded, *Have you seen*
 that latest viral cat clip? We showed it to our aunts and they

put down the pills that time. And lo the beast lumbered
 back from whence it came, zipping

up the portal. As it shuffled off it said,
 Number five really did get me. Go in peace,

my child. We quickly wipe a tear
 and snap a selfie, hashtag Best Life. Hashtag

Didn't Get Destroyed.
 Hashtag Super Blessed.

Adaptable

What grows in a city: adaptable gardens
        and determined weeds. Verdant manes

erupting from the shelves of old concrete. Like
        this, we leave apartments and conveyor

down the streets. We guard our bodies
        closely, like, *Wands up, earbuds in.* Press

our lips together, our majestic resting bitch face.
        Know that if we don't talk, it might not be

you. It might be that one guy glanced
        our bare thighs when we did. Know that

if we don't grin, it might be
        we don't want to. It might be that one

guy who screamed, *But you were flirting.* When
        all we did was smile and turn

down his pick-up line. Things that we have
        Googled: *Shirt that says "Don't talk to me."*

Things that we have Googled: *I feel like screaming
        all of the time.* Things that we have Googled:

Does this count? Does that count? Things that we
        have Googled: *Discount resources for grief.*

Faith

Our families tease us
for checking the locks twice,

walking with keys splicing out
of our hands like knockoff Wolverines, but

we cannot extract them
from our minds: editorials

on the women whose bodies
were found in ravines,

robbed of their breathing,
cut from their life. The women

who messaged with the men for months,
who didn't rush in, who picked

public meet-ups, who told all their friends
what time they expected to be home. *She did*

everything right, they say. *She didn't
miss a thing.*

Tarot Reading for the End of the World

Two of Wands

Discoveries, the card says. They are not created equal. That we can't wander fountain-side shopping malls at night due to windowless vans and the things that take place there. That the things that take place there are worse than we imagined. That goodness is not armor. That goodness is no shield. That we talk about the good things we do in the Uber, the volunteer work, the courteous things, praying that the driver will not throw the auto-lock and speed off into an alley. That we need to celebrate so much more carefully. That confetti is both spangle and gag. That when the teacher had us all release balloons on Earth Day—what was she thinking?—several things most likely died.

Princess of Pentacles (reversed)

Slothfulness, the card says. Wanting all for nothing. Wanting to uproot whole systems like thorned weeds. *You haven't paid your due diligence,* they chide us. *You haven't put in your 3-5 years.* We say, But *this is entry-level stuff—people are dying!* Rattling the cages while they sip brandy and smile. Humans made systems and humans can undo them. That's the idea, but we only live so long. These heart-arms are carrying groceries and interest rates, part-time jobs and chronic pain and midnight coffee howls. These heart-arms are buckling, elbows jelly-quivering, spiral-eyed emojis peeking out from kale fronds. Every generation has wanted something different. We know this, but we see the sword of Damocles, its gleam. If adolescence is the refusal to claim *normal,* then indeed, we are stunted as you say.

Temperance (reversed)

Excess, the card says. Let alcohol flow through the streets like a bacchanal river. Let us light cigars off of dollar bills. Succumb—if you can't beat them, join them. Let palms like jeweled gauntlets pat our backs behind closed doors: *You know how it is. This is just the game, kid.* Insisting that hierarchies bend and flex but do not break. That they reincarnate as something else—a game of hide-and-go-seek. Let us shelter ourselves and nothing else; let us barricade our bodies. Let no harm come unto us and we'll tune the static out. Shut the blinds as Vesuvius coats whole neighborhoods in red. Healthcare for a promise not to look at those burnt bodies. Just sign here. We say, *Wait.* We say, *No.*

GEODE-EATERS

We who crack the geode crack the purple splinters too. We who cannot contain contentment only one tier deep. We who seek something other than gemstones—we seek the light within them. We seek the circling molecules that shift like drifting fish. Orange and all asparkle, glimmer dimmer as they fade. We ache to follow through the portal unto truths unseen. We who are not content with the geode, cannot be content with the geode. We who seek a rupturing of geodes altogether. We know—the inner surface is a childlike placation. This world needs more than gentle buffing, more than vigorous polishing. Needs, requires overhaul. Our blood hears starlight in these stones. We want to crack and drink it. To swallow opal nectar, let its milk run down our chins.

Apotropaic

We have read all the stories. Little Red
        getting gobbled, Sleeping Beauty's

finger pricked, Snow White choking on
        a sweet fruit laced with venom. We know

all that preys on an obstinate mind—liars,
        opportunists, and the envious, the cold. Fairy tale

monsters hiding under our beds with
        names broadcast from billboards and screens,

ensconced in immaculate thrones. A spectacle,
        a dizzying, this cavalcade of

want. And *to want*, we are told,
        is divine. We have read all the

theories on the Sheela Na Gig,
        the sculptures of women holding open their bodies

and beaming, found in churches, spent
        cathedrals, under pews. *A warning,* some say, *against*

hungering flesh. Some say, *A compromise: ancient*
        religion melding with the new. What we like best

is the one that says, *Graffiti. Fertility cultists*
        thumbing their noses at pious invaders, no doubt. All

our books on witchcraft (bought used on eBay)
        say customization will enhance an object's power. This

is why we love old things, dented, battered—in other words,
    customized by the world, by time and damage's knife. This

is why we carve our own graffiti—a whittled doll,
    a loaf of bread we kneaded with our hands. This

is why we bring them to each other, walking past
    the Big Box drenched in slogans, even if we bought

the ingredients there. This is our defiance, our small act
    of creation—a collaging, a reworking of parts. Even if

it is an enormous machine, a titan that carries
    our want and our will, we'll be the ripped-jean ghosts

on its back. A network
    of fuchsia in gray. Apotropaic—

a ward against evil.
    A talisman locked in a fist.

Morals

We shake the old stories
      like hourglasses, like

kaleidoscopes. *Don't talk to*
      strangers, for they might be

wolves, or *Huntsmen will always*
      save you? Like, *Always expand*

your party invites, or *Beware*
      selfish queens? Like, *Don't*

succumb to vanity, or *Kisses*
      always heal? What is the moral

in our bones—no, written in
      our rib cage? *God helps those*

who help themselves, or *This*
      whole thing is screwed?

If this world is a story,
      what is its moral?

That depends—are we
      the sovereign or the heir?

Ordinary Magic

Wireless connections are always going down when we're stressed and working under deadline. The coffee shop managers rustle the routers, rub the backs of their necks in confusion. Add to that streetlamps are always snapping off when we wander softly beneath them. These glaring spotlights, their glow paints a circle on concrete until we approach. A flipped-off switch—the show's plug pulled. It used to bother us, but now we agree that things are more honest in the dark. Such ordinary magic—just enough to put a bounce in our sneakered step, just enough to feel special. But parlor tricks—can they topple chronic empire? Do our small stories tip the scales? Can beings electrified from universe sockets, all buzzing, rechannel that lightning? Tell us—what kind of narrative is this?

Narratives

The kind of narrative where the villainous triumph,
    cackling on railroad tracks.
The kind of narrative where the lovers reunite,
    collapsing to knees with relief.
The kind of narrative where the small and the powerful
    oust the big and the bad.
The kind of narrative where the effort is admonished with a slow clapping
    of hands.
The kind of narrative where the heroes are tricked into brutally impaling
    one another.
The kind of narrative where illusion lifts and the princess recovers
    her crown.
The kind of narrative where rain washes the ruins of a city.
The kind of narrative where the values are different: we call this "utopia."
The kind of narrative where the knights don't let their palms be greased
    with silver.
The kind of narrative where the orphaned child doesn't know his strength.
The kind of narrative where animals and humans always harm each other.
The kind of narrative where animals and humans, sometimes, can get along.
The kind of narrative where the weak are pillaged by the roving chariots.
The kind of narrative where thriving is seen as a contest, not a right.
The kind of narrative where tyrants swirl homes like stirring coffee.
The kind of narrative where everyone thinks that nothing is wrong, but
    really something is.
The kind of narrative where oceans rise and swallow up whole coastlines.
The kind of narrative where lies and deception get more clicks than truth.
The kind of narrative where extinction is occasionally met with a chortling
    womp womp.
The kind of narrative where our bleakest hour becomes meme-ified.
The kind of narrative where we want to, want to, want to hack the
    source code.
The kind of narrative where we watch in slow motion, hit rewind, hit play.
The kind where we don't know what else to do, and so we just hit play.

Embedded

How do you combat
>　or reform something

of which you are
>　a part? How do you aim

for the heart of a thunderous
>　titan while gripping its back?

Our dark night drives, our laughter
>　out windows are all embedded in this.

Our proms and our pets
>　and our jeans and our gifts

wrapped in polyethylene. When every
>　heroic rope-swing from rafters

lands us right back here? Is this
>　a closed circle—an endless hoop smooth

as the insides of keychains we nervously thumb?
>　Is our ability to envision something new

dependent on what contact
>　lenses we can afford? Tell us, just what

do we bring to a duel
>　when the whole room is made of swords?

Thread 1

Text—i'm grateful
for each morning
in the maw with u.

finding ur hair
in the crease of my pillow
causes me to thank the sky.

Text—the sky that ripples
with the glossy blip of ozone
shrinkage. *static* & the leap

of record warping, slurring
notes. ur last image
didn't come through, but

Text—i'm glad
u sent it. *static* &
the concert pauses with

a raised baton. i'm sure
there were drums just a moment
ago. i'm sure i heard violas.

Text—can u resend
that last one? all i got
was hand, egg, fire, &

the laugh-cry face. here's
a gif of icebergs cracking back
into an ocean. here's a pic of

Text—that time
we climbed
the old pine tree.

Text—i didn't
get ur message. *static
static static.*

Text—my circuits
are unfurling, like
a mountain peeling rind.

Text—the party was
exquisite. talk to u
next time.

Fortress

Fever Dream

Our curtains on rented balconies part,
fluttering feathers

that echo the moon. We step
onto concrete four stories up

and weave between succulents planted
in ribbed cans abandoned by Folgers

grounds. The gloam is all ashimmer. We blink—
it is all gossamer, translucent indigo. *Just think*

happy thoughts, a voice croons. Siri or Alexa. Or some
other lady robot styled to seduce. Our bare

heels levitate as wind brushes our cheeks. We think
of homemade cocktails, sprigs of rosemary bridging

their rims. We think of calling an ambulance
instead of an Uber when we gash ourselves

hand-washing our knives. *Not like that,* the robot
chuckles. Our trajectory corrects as we soar

over downtown, its towers rigid fingers
specked with diamond flakes. A glitter, a colossus reaching

up. So we imagine gorging on caviar and champagne,
buying Boardwalk and seeding red hotels upon its throat.

We imagine plugging our last tuppence in the bank—
to hell with feeding pigeons!—hail railways and dams!

Lady robot sighs, contented, plays our favorite dance
track. We sail by the alleyways where dumpster scavengers

flinch. We sail by the suburbs, where the minivans
are sleeping. We sail by the gas stations, where beer

signs flicker blue. The teenage nightshift cashier shivers,
squints up on her smoke break. *Do not fret,*

says lady robot. *She cannot see you. These are but shadows
of what was, what is, and what shall be. I entered*

this story late, so please, do not blame me. Out we sail
down the freeway, cornfields lashing cobalt. Phone

lines like immense incisions, silhouette and hum. Out
past slaughterhouses, where the blood runs into

rivers. Out past ranches where the workers jolt
from their nightmares. Hands that pump the factories

hot—trembling with sweat. Out past
the grandpas stroking rosaries in barnyards. Out past

the forests where the raccoon tails dart. Where crickets chirp and
glinting eyes and snuffles forge a cloak. *We can't*

stay here, warns lady robot, seeing us press our palms
to bark and bask in dewy coldness. We become vapor, rising up

above the canopy. Above the telephone poles and above
the shifting cirrus clouds. We pass through jets, watch

travelers who watch their tiny screens. From up here, the city—
a gallon of sparks cascaded onto darkness. Thousands of offices

holding humans striving to do well. *Hark,* the robot says.
Our master. System angel. Lord. The nightscape shifts—a shoulder

blade bedecked in homes and roads. It walks—a massive
titan holding industries and zip codes. Humans striving

to hold on. Their frantic, typing hands. Moss and cattle
tumble from its shuddering momentum. Rusted buildings snap

like twigs and crunch beneath its feet. *This is the pale
blue dot,* says lady robot, zooming us out further. Pulling us, as if

by cord, into the violet void. We see it—Earth, a pinprick
in a beam of peony glow. Bright and small as beach sand caught

between index and thumb. *Please select a filter
for this image,* her voice urges. *It's just begging*

*for an inspirational quote in all caps font. Or swipe left
if you don't like it—we can take another. This*

*too is replaceable. I'm sure
we still have time.*

Word of the Year

In 2015, Oxford Dictionaries named the "Face with Tears of Joy" emoji the word of the year, stating that it "best reflected the ethos, mood, and preoccupations" of the time.

We had a feel the other day
and heavens, was it noxious.

We texted each other, *I'm
having a feel. It might be more*

than one. Feels—the unmitigated
contraptions alarming in

our chests. Red beating
and thundering, cacophony

and surge. We wanted to
do something, *say* something,

touch something, *hold* something,
revel embodied. WebMD

says it might be contagious, so please
cover your mouth. Honestly, cover it;

swallow your tongue. We don't
have time to play counselor. Send us

"Face with Tears of Joy" and
we will send you ours.

Shrug

Language
fails. Gawky and

abashed, we fumble
meaning. All that falls

down cracks
and storm drains is

our hope for this.
By this, we mean

a ladder out. A manhole.
In other words, ¯_(ツ)_/¯.

Personality Test

SHARE YOUR REACTIONS TO THE FOLLOWING STATEMENTS. KEEP TRACK OF YOUR ANSWERS TO LEARN ABOUT YOURSELF!

1. In 2018 / military spending / around the world / topped $1.7 trillion. / A giant claw / poised atop a wall / and pushing, / pushing it down. / This is what it means / to top something— / to transcend it, to crumble it / back to powder, / to rubble it / back to dust.

a. Like   b. Love   c. Haha   d. Wow   e. Sad   f. Angry

2. In 1987 / a researcher catalogued / and analyzed euphemisms / commonly used in discussions of atomic weapons. / Words that are sequined / to mask the thing's face. / *Christmas tree.* / *Cookie cutter.* / *Marry up.* / She calls this *nuclear language.*

a. Like   b. Love   c. Haha   d. Wow   e. Sad   f. Angry

3. In 2008 / the United Nations wagered / solving global hunger was a doable goal. / A representative claimed $30 billion / a year could surely / end it. / Scientists balked about the number / of dollars and also the number / of mouths. Plenty / of articles quibbled this point. It all became very / abstract.

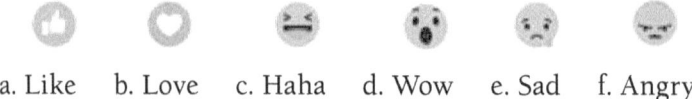

a. Like   b. Love   c. Haha   d. Wow   e. Sad   f. Angry

4. In 2010 / PepsiCo offered / a biodegradable bag. Concerned that litter / was unintentional marketing— / a bad image problem— / they wrapped their SunChips in plant-based satchels and smiled their PepsiCo / smiles. People complained / the wrappers were too loud and sales / began to plummet. PepsiCo swiftly withdrew / the bag. This happened / in under a year.

a. Like   b. Love   c. Haha   d. Wow   e. Sad   f. Angry

5. There is no puzzle, / no video game, / more difficult than / this world. We turn it / and turn it / in our hands. We hold it / to the light. Some want to see / inside it so badly / they sometimes consider / the hammer. Such glitter there / must be inside. So many / working parts.

a. Like   b. Love   c. Haha   d. Wow   e. Sad   f. Angry

DON'T FORGET TO COUNT UP YOUR ANSWERS!

KEY:

If you answered mostly...

a. Congrats! Very little / will change.

b. Congrats! Very little / will change.

c. Congrats! Very little / will change.

d. Congrats! Very little / will change.

e. Congrats! Very little / will change.

f. Congrats! Very little / will change.

The Age of the Image

The thought was
        in the age of the image

these things would not
        continue. In seeing them

we would extinguish them,
        eradicate the ills. Still we sit

by our moms as they weep
        over big game gunned

in awareness videos. Awareness. What
        if we are aware? We are all so very

aware now. What if awareness
        is not the balm? Will never be

the correct salve? We shut
        down the monitor, say,

Don't worry—maybe it
        was staged.

Paywall

The article says, "Don't fear!
There's hope! If we all just—"

then we were
paywalled.

Moloch 1

Cow-faced god, thorny
-headed one aglimmer,

cactus-armed and curl-
browed, enormity of gold—

that *idol* were only a moniker
for falsity; that *idol* did not connote epic

role model too. *The strongest
and the fiercest* made *fiercer*

by despair, says Milton—he paints you a warrior;
a fallen angel rebel; a tragic, rain-spattered

rock star. *Open war,* he has you
summon. *Sulfur and strange fire.* These are lines

from action movies, chased by guitar
screams. Moloch, we can almost see

your discount action figure—"Now with jaws
that really chew!"—beneath the Christmas tree.

And what was that line again? *Endless oil
and stone? Moloch whose soul is electricity and banks?* Even

before Ginsberg, what was that gray fever
dream? In Lang's hands, a drooling mouth,

a ravenous machine. Hissing and spitting
your hot steam from shined valves, scalding

the buttons on men's coats. Moloch, you've been
passed around, a talking point at therapy, an heirloom

inherited, like it
or not. Whole words have been invented

meaning "death from overwork." In multiple
languages. Your tendril paws expand. What

was that line again? *I saw the best minds
of my generation* sell their blood plasma

for rent? What was that ad again? *You're never going
to be able to retire—why should your boots?* Fill us

in, Moloch. We haven't had internet
since last week, and the café is kicking us out.

Moloch 2

Moloch ✓ @Moloch9000 •10m

PPL OF EARTH! I speak now 2 u from the altar of ur time. I am wrapping my hands around ur throat—no, don't worry!—to straighten ur tie. To give u a pearl necklace. To cup the back of ur neck for a kiss. U see, I just adore u. I just cannot stay away.

💬 9.1K   🔁 45K   ♡ 162K   ✉

Moloch ✓ @Moloch9000 •5m

The ppl who tell u I am a villain are BAD, BAD PPL—THE WORST! I've had 2 block several ppl already who claimed I devoured their children. If children wander in 2 my mouth, I can't be responsible, can I? I am an old-world god. Remorse just doesn't go w/ gold.

💬 4.6K   🔁 21K   ♡ 90K   ✉

Moloch ✓ @Moloch9000 •20s

PPL OF ERTH, I'm humbled by ur support about the children. Ppl today want 2 pass the buck, want 2 sprinkle blame like birdseed. I'll be posting the names/addresses of ppl who harassed me. I'm not one 2 advocate violence. I'm just saying maybe the Invisible Hand can wield a knife.

💬 903   🔁 5.9K   ♡ 16K   ✉

Personhood

In 2018
Domino's Pizza
helped cities pave
their roads.

The remedied
potholes glistened
with spray-painted logos
and language: *Oh yes*

we did. If most
people are lovable,
does that
include our

friendly
neighborhood
corporate
overlords?

By this
we mean: is this
the new
paternalistic grip?

Offers we
cannot refuse
with sides of steaming
breadsticks?

Offers we
should leave
five-star reviews,
our tear-soaked thanks?

Made for You

We slouch in the fire
        escape, having failed

to change the world
        again. Loneliness eats

our hearts like a vulture
        tearing a carcass clean.

We let the corporation
        win today. We boot up

the playlist Spotify made
        us based on our recent

listens. Algorithms are not
        the same thing as caring,

but the program knows
        us so well. And maybe

the coder lovingly tending
        the code is a kind of caring,

right? A care crossing
        distances to reach our ears.

ONLINE FORUM

Question:

I'm afraid of everything
        all the time

and I can't for the life of me
        get a diagnosis.

The doctor says it's normal,
        that nothing is wrong—

that I just need more
        self-help talk

and maybe a new shirt. *Retail*
        therapy, she says.

Am I
        wrong?

Answer:

I'm afraid of everything
        all the time too,

but my doctor says
        it's just me.

That war and devastation
        will always be with us,

like Jesus said the poor
        will always be here too.

Poorness and peace
    be with you, I guess.

He prescribed me three
    kinds of anti-depressants—

I'll mail you some
    if you like.

Boss Fight

When the fog rolls in like this—
when the mist pearls our eyelashes
and everything is cellophane hung
-over gray, and the streets shine impressionist
with turquoise and umber, and the screens
on our windows shudder chainmail lace—
we would will our hands to glow, as if in
a boss fight, as if we were sorcerers. With days left
until the next direct deposit, we refresh,
refresh the app. Thumbs a kind of approximate
glimmer. A battery at ten percent. We snack
on jam and soup crackers. We stroke our sleeping
cats. We hurl our scarves around ourselves
and head out into morning. As if it is
a tired war, an automated bluster. As if it is
a kind of scabbard, us a yielding blade. Onslaught
slow as condensation—struggle,
not so much.

Shortcuts

We Ctrl+F the bodies
of digital texts: emails,

webpages, Word documents.
We search for what eludes

our eye, the vital characters.
We wish we could Ctrl+F

the bodies of our lovers,
scan them for haecceity,

if such a thing exists. Essential
them-ness, core of their make

-up. Where this might
reside. In lung or spleen

or fingertip. Or nestled under
valve. We wish we could

lift up the tablets, slim screens
drawing in sudden glass glare,

hit the camera button and
on this, hit Ctrl+F. Find

what we are looking for, so
easy now, so clean.

Thread 2

Text—stand on
this platform with me

static
        static

even tho the city is a
gnashing of jaws.

even if the gale
blows the petals from

our rafters. even if there are
no heroes here.

Text—look downward at
the illuminated crunching.

an altar, a ceremonial
knife. a bloodletting,

a *static*. even if our hands
cannot glow and conjure

lightning to push back, well,
they can get a little warm. if we hold

them together, they can get a little
warmer. so hold them, please

Text—hold mine.

SIEGE

Through the Cracks

There is depth in the city
if you look through the cracks,

a slumbering wreath
of magnolia blossoms

shivering with bees. It is
gold gold gold and a

stir and a hum and now look:
it is just waking up—

Blossoming 1

On these evenings our heads tilt
up and become flowers, busting
out of our collars, all iridescent.
Geranium, freesia, gladiolus
erupting straight out of our
used T-shirts. With smartphones in
our pockets—our long winter
coats. Our cheeks shift to
druzy, a spiked hymn of glitter
refracting and clutching
the siren-scraped light. The red
-green-yellow *No Vacancy* din. We
are all wind, all magenta. Our laughter
a rooftop vertigo, a circle of lips
on a bottle's swan neck. Geode
heartbeats keeping time. A wallowing,
a daisy in cement.

BLOSSOMING 2

On these evenings
we tip
our mouths
to the star line
and drink
and drink
and drink.
We are universe
flowers, roiling
with oil spill
luster, all
dazzled with
pop-rocking
glint. Hum
a kind of static
that crescendoes,
splitting walls.

The Squeeze

If the depth of our love
is proportional to

the breadth and extent
of our leisure time,

it's a miracle our hands
can stop typing long enough

to interlace at dusk. The
Squeeze, some call it. That lifting

our eyes is a signal
of refutation. That taking

a walk as the sky burns
lavender is an act of war. We breathe

though invisible waters are rising
upward toward our sternums. Breathe

though the hillcrest is fading
now, succumbing green to gloam.

Advice

We flail in aquatic rupture—
spiraling, a suction—beating green

and swirling blue with open
palms and soles. This is what they call

Charybdis, drowned instead of eaten:
preferable, a free choice, we guess—a result

of supply and demand. In their golden
ships they watch us, flanked by orange life vests.

Flanked by rafts and inflatable rings
and ropes and water jugs. They cup their hands

around their mouths. They wave to get
our attention. They flash their grins at us,

manicured pearls. *Bootstraps!*
they holler. *Bootstraps!*

Discordant

We have read all the stories and we know
the conductors are leering menacingly.

Their ascots and perfectly tailored tuxedos
cannot conceal their fangs. Upbraiding us, now,

to take our seats—they tap the music stands.
We wanted to trust them like shiny-eyed wizards

from tales we were told. Guardians, mentors
advising initiate trembling to calm and steel.

We wanted so badly to trust them, to lean on
their wisdom, their knowledge of pathways. Wanted

to feel their hands on our shoulders were
not poised to give us a shove. Generation-eaters,

our lips unglue from our horns. The song you command
is a death march and we cannot play the notes.

Suspicion

We know the thing is nice and also
know the thing is deadly. Fairy tale bargain—

sorry, we were raised on these. "Give up
your hands and I'll give you these

gloves. Such quality—softest
kid skin." No. We see the glittering

knife in your pocket. Smell
the blood on your breath.

Datum

When you lie here, cat—
        and your whiskers twitch

and your river rock toes
        retract raptor-curved claws

except for the slate crescent
        tips we can see, and your belly

hair rises, polished and warm,
        in a sun slat bounced off of

corporate windows blinking
        across the alley—when you flick

your tail in bounding dreams
        and pivot your ear to the screech

of a starling perched on a
        telephone wire—then we remember

that you are the product of
        everything that came before you: entire

dramas, whole eons of cats, that you
        are what they have led to. Pocket of heritage,

aggregate genes. A datum
        that cannot be stored.

Unpreservable precious thing—
        a thrown arc that cannot be stilled.

Museums

Use the blood of the redwoods
to needle our skin a tapestry of iris.

Carve them up
and down our spines. Our bones,

our fertile flesh. We would bear them,
we would wear them: indelible

refuge of what screams under
boot soles. What violet petals turned

velvet pulp, what residue of greed. Cover
our eyelids with amethyst; adorn us

with drenched seaweed. Dye our clothes
with the juices of rivers. Fold us up in

incarnadine briar. We will carry the ghosts
of what is lost, make shelters of

our bodies. Become custom jobs; become
living museums, encyclopedic weight.

Trivia

We trace each other's tattoos
of flora and fauna—a squirrel,

a mallard duck's opulent throat,
vast tidal waves swallowing elbows—

in the window seats of breakfast nooks
painted sanatorium white. Drizzle

drizzles the overpass yawn and the stern
architecture of industry shuts its face

like a slumbering gargoyle. On phones
we pull up frogs as bright as pirates'

rubies, duchesses' emeralds. Try to say
their names in Latin. Try to prove

some point. This is how we know
these things for beer-stained trivia

answer sheets. This is how we know
these things that we have never held.

So the story of the thing
and not the thing is treasured,

cherished like a fairy tale,
concept over pulse.

Communion with Nature

The majority of living beings
        cannot be touched. Just witnessed

via pixels. We are the wildest
        creatures our fingers can brush, no

polar bears. No tigers padding
        verdant tilth. No chartreuse Luna

moths. We are the breathing,
        the undulate rib cage, the eyelash

laced with moon. We pray to the patron
        saint of organic matter, *Cushion*

these organs. Pray to the patron protector
        of arteries, *Let it all flow on.* We touch

each other and ourselves and this
        is communion with nature. Biology

binding to land more eternal
        than all that is built on its hull. This

is a certain method of
        agency: lullaby elegy power.

Prayer

Dear chomping chasm,
please help us all

adult sufficiently today.
Dear void of starlight,

please help the young ones
who call this *the best*

of all dull dystopias. Please
help us face our untreated

second shadows, the monsters
that echo our footsteps

on tile, that hover
there, silent and needing.

Please help our small hands
on keyboards produce

something of value. Of value
to someone other than simply

the whirlpool, vacuous
stock exchange. Please save

a little for when we get home;
please help us keep our charge

that long. Please bring dreams
of consequences; help

us be
that brave.

Thread 3

Iron groans through the glimmering
haze, steel beams a sighing. A feat

of mechanical marvels, city sacramental
awe. More palatable than rosy glows

of elemental dawning. This: constructed
bounty from the harvest of the gloom.

A trophy bestowed unto ourselves, a brash,
intoxicating spoil. Something whose hide

seeps spores that choke our stunned alveoli.
When hazardous materials have been released

into the atmosphere, we lock and bolt
our doors. Select *a small, interior room*

like ones that breathe and bleed. Like ones
we rent in sunken pits beneath the busy

highways. Ones we cling to, pale blue
dots in strands of passing light. We shelter

in these places—*a precaution, a precaution*—
we hope will keep us safe. We hold hands

and hold our pets. We listen to good
tidings; we peek at the searing sun.

We have read all the stories and we know
this narrative is a kind uncertain. We shelter

in place—
in place—because

where else are we going
to shelter?

*

*

*

*

*

*

*

*

*

*

*

*

*

*

*

*

*

*

*

*

*

*

*

*

*

*

*

*

*

*

*

static

static

static

Text—

There is depth in the city—
opalescent, oceanic churning.

Song that widens splintered
fissures: structural hazard.

Words aquiver on our tongues
are pushing concrete open,

petals issued from our hands
defiant, taking root—

Apotropaic: a shelter against
this whirlwind, this cyclone.

Shelter open just a crack
to let each other in—

NOTES

The line "The city is enough with us" in "Candle and Laptop" is inspired by "The World Is Too Much with Us" by William Wordsworth. It is dedicated to my parents' cat, who disappeared on Halloween in the 1980s.

"Fever Dream" references *Peter Pan* by J. M. Barrie; *A Christmas Carol* by Charles Dickens; the Walt Disney film *Mary Poppins*, as well as G. R. Sims' *Living London*, on which the film's song "Fidelity Fiduciary Bank" is based; and *Pale Blue Dot* by Carl Sagan, as well as the photograph of Earth taken by Voyager 1 on which that book's title is based. It also references the fact that factory farm workers frequently experience post-traumatic stress disorder, as reported by *The Texas Observer* and others, and the fact Uber is emerging as an alternative to ambulances, as reported by *NPR* and others.

The essay referenced in "Personality Test" is "Slick 'Ems, Glick 'Ems, Christmas Trees, and Cookie Cutters: Nuclear Language and How We Learned to Pat the Bomb" by Carol Cohn. Other figures and events are inspired by articles such as "Global Military Spending Remains High at $1.7 Trillion" by the Stockholm International Peace Research Institute, "UN Says Solving Food Crisis Could Cost $30 Billion" by *The New York Times,* and "Snack Attack: Chip Eaters Make Noise About a Crunchy Bag" by *The Wall Street Journal.*

Italicized portions of "Moloch 1" are drawn from *Paradise Lost* by John Milton, "Howl" by Allen Ginsberg, and a 2017 Timberland advertisement. Also referenced is Fritz Lang's film *Metropolis.*

As of the writing of "Moloch 2," there was no actual Twitter user named @Moloch9000. This is a fictional account.

For one example of an article that discusses the potholes mentioned in "Personhood," see "Why Domino's Pizza is Fixing Potholes Now" in *CityLab.*

The line "the story of the thing and not the thing" in "Trivia" is inspired by the line "the wreck and not the story of the wreck / the thing itself and not the myth" by Adrienne Rich in her poem "Diving into the Wreck."

The idea of the "dull dystopia" mentioned in "Prayer" is inspired by conversations I had with the students in my ENGL 102 class, Spring 2018.

CATHERINE KYLE grew up in Seattle and currently lives in Boise. Her other collections include *Coronations, Saint: A Post-Dystopian Hagiography, Parallel, Gamer: A Role-Playing Poem, Flotsam,* and *Feral Domesticity.* Her writing has been honored by the Idaho Commission on the Arts, the Alexa Rose Foundation, and other organizations. She is an assistant professor of English at the College of Western Idaho and also teaches for The Cabin. Her website is catherinebaileykyle.com.

www.ingramcontent.com/pod-product-compliance
Lightning Source LLC
Chambersburg PA
CBHW020130130526
44591CB00032B/582